I0568677

THE TRUTH OF THE

RESURRECTION

OF JESUS CHRIST

By

Edgardo Samaniego

COPYRIGHT © EDGARDO SAMANIEGO

BSC; DIPLOMA OF BUSINESS

ABN: 42714813139

Dedication

I sincerely dedicate this book to all humanity. I want the whole world to really know what Jesus Christ did when he was down here on earth for a short period of time. He revealed to the world the true nature and will of the Almighty Father God—the omnipotence, omniscience, omnipresence, love, mercy, and attributes of God.

Acknowledgment

I deeply appreciate and acknowledge the creator of the Urantia Book and the Urantia Book Foundation for giving the book to the world.

The book that revealed the truth about God, the whole Universe and Universes' creations. The book testifies the whole creations of universes, its planets, suns, moons, satellites, and all its living things and beings of plants, animals, humans, and the evolutionary panorama of it all.

Contents

FOREWORD

The truth about the real reason for the crucifixion and death of Jesus Christ was written in the bible, but in a different way. The truth is Jesus Christ laid down his life according to his own free will, and he also had the divine and absolute power to take it up again.

When Jesus was sentenced to death on the cross by the high priest of the Sanhedrin, and to be executed by the Roman Soldiers, he had all the complete power to avoid that kind of horrible death by sending his legions of angels to purge all the people who wanted him dead.

Jesus Christ also did not die to pay for the sins of the whole world. The false belief that God the Father sacrificed the life of his only begotten son to pay for the sin of the world. This is the most repulsive insult to the omnipotent, omniscient, omnipresent, most loving, most merciful and forgiving God. This belief is extremely primitive, barbaric and ignorant. The Universal Father did not owe anything to anyone. Actually, the whole world and the universe owe everything to the Universal Father.

The truth is, Jesus Christ came down to the world as flesh and blood, lived like a normal human being for the divine purpose of declaring, demonstrating and manifesting to the whole world the true attributes, nature, love and mercy of the Universal Father. Jesus was human and divine. Jesus is the Son of Man and the Son of God.

Jesus lived and died for the whole universe and not just for a certain race on earth. He demonstrated that death is a real part of mortal existence. Jesus clearly demonstrated that there is life after death and that life is eternal.

Jesus Christ showed, demonstrated and gave the world his absolute love and mercy, and he did not ask for anything in return but to have complete faith and trust in the Universal Father, which he manifested during his short sojourn on Urantia (Earth).

The believers must not selfishly care and desire much of their personal salvation, but rather follow the life and teaching of Jesus, who showed unselfish love and desire to serve other fellows. Jesus showed his love to the world, he loves his family; friends, associates and he even loves his enemy.

Human believers, non-believers, all creatures must love one another and remove their feelings of hypocrisy, selfishness and self-righteousness.

Jesus Christ was crucified and died or was killed on the cross on Friday afternoon. And before he was crucified, he told his disciples that he will rise again on the third day. Some believed, but most are skeptical.

The Sanhedrin, the Pharisees and Sadducees are worried, so they went to Pilate to ask for extra guards to station outside the tomb of Joseph. They sent ten Roman guards plus ten Jewish guards to station outside the tomb of Joseph Arimathea, where Jesus' body was laid inside. They even put another stone and the seal of Pilate outside the tomb. They fully secured the tomb and made sure that no one could get in and out of the tomb and take the body of Jesus away. They guarded the tomb full time, 24 hours a day.

On the third day, Sunday morning, Mary Magdalene was the first person to find the tomb empty. She cried and thought the body had been stolen. Mary Magdalene was the first person whose resurrected body appeared. Jesus' morontia being appeared to Mary Magdalene outside the tomb.

THE RESURRECTION

Urantia Book Paper 189

Soon after the burial of Jesus on Friday afternoon, the chief of the archangels of Nebadon, then present on Urantia, summoned his council of the resurrection of sleeping will creatures and entered upon the consideration of a possible technique for the restoration of Jesus.

Some of the angels of the local universe of Nebadon are concerned about their Lord Jesus, that they assembled to try to do something to resurrect their Sovereign Lord, Michael of Nebadon. But Gabriel, the Chief Executive, advises them that Michael (Jesus Christ) has the absolute will and power to lay down his life, and he also has the complete authority and power to raise it up again.

The Personalized Adjuster of Jesus separated from the personality of Jesus and became the temporary director and spokesperson for Jesus during his temporary sleep. The Personalized Adjuster of Jesus, who is also in command of the celestial hosts stationed on Urantia (earth), spoke to them that no creatures of the Creator-Father ought to assist or be involved in any way in the process of resurrection.

No creatures of material and spiritual beings can help to rise up the creator. Michael bestowed himself to become as Jesus, a mortal of flesh and blood on earth. Jesus Christ chose freely the bestowal experience to become mortal of the realm and experience the life of a mortal being for thirty-six years. His mission has the full blessing from the Universal Father. Jesus Christ has the complete power and authority to lay down his life, and he also has the full authority, power and control to take it up again.

As creatures, you can only observe the whole divine and glorious undertaking of the Creator of the local universe, to experience to live as a mortal of the world, experience a horrible death, and rise from the mortal death to morontia resurrection, then restoring himself to full spiritual being with all his eternal and glorious power and authority over the universe and universes and all its will creatures.

THE MORONTIA TRANSIT

Paper 189:1

At two forty-five Sunday morning, the Paradise Incarnation Commission, consisting of seven unidentified Paradise personalities, arrived on the scene and immediately deployed around the tomb.

At the very early hours of Sunday morning, before three am, there was a strange event that was transpiring inside Joseph Arimathea's tomb, where the body of Jesus was laid. An extreme vibration, blinding bright light and extraordinary phenomena occurring inside the tomb resulted in the appearance of the resurrected morontia form and personality of Jesus of Nazareth, who came out from the tomb of Joseph. This divine and glorious incident happened on April 9, A.D. 30.

Jesus' resurrected body of morontia form is outside the tomb, and Jesus' material body of flesh and blood, who died on the cross, is still lying inside the tomb, undisturbed and still wrapped in a linen sheet as it has been since Friday afternoon. But this lifeless body of Jesus in the sepulcher niche was just a discarded shell that had no connection to the risen Christ, the Creator Son of the local universe. The guards have not even had the slightest idea of what was transpiring that early morning inside the tomb. The stone outside the entrance to the tomb is still intact; the seal of Pilate is still untouched. The ten Jewish guards and the ten Roman guards are still watching attentively outside the tomb without any suspicion of what just happened inside the tomb.

The believers, even to this day and age, still believe that Jesus' resurrection is material (physical). That Jesus' whole body of flesh and blood ascended to heaven. The world must understand and carefully discern what Jesus is always saying in his teaching that "my kingdom is not of this world." God is spirit, his sons and all his heavenly associates and coordinates are spirit beings. They live in spiritual spheres, not in material and evolutionary worlds. Christ Michael came down on earth as a babe of Bethlehem. Lived and died as a normal mortal being. But he is a spirit being, a Creator Son.

Christ Michael became human Jesus of a physical and mortal body; to commune, live, teach, demonstrate the love, mercy, forgiveness and glory of the Universal Father. And after around thirty-six years of his life on earth, which he chose to return to his father in heaven in a way that all mortal beings will experience in life, death of the physical body, (physical to morontial to spiritual), then to finally attain eternal life.

There are three forms of beings in the universe and universes;

1) The material or physical being- the being of flesh of blood. This being belongs only to the physical world, and it will remain in the material world. Ashes to ashes, dust to dust.

2) The Morontia being – the being between material and spiritual. (The Soul). This is the stage of progressive evolvement from material to spiritual.

3) The Spirit being – this being is the ultimate and absolute goal of the evolutionary being. From mere material mortal to morontia being, finally to spiritual being that is eternal and infinite.

After Jesus had risen from the tomb, and greeted Gabriel and his angels waiting for him outside the tomb. He gave instructions to Gabriel to administer the universe's affairs and extend regards and brotherly love to Immanuel, (Christ Michael, Brother in Heavenly spheres). He also organizes all involved, like the Most High of Edentia and the Ancient of Days, as to his transition from morontia form to a full and original spirit being. He advised them all that he would still tarry on earth in Morontia, being to commune with his mortal associates for a few days to continue his teaching of revealing the will of the Heavenly Father to the world.

Jesus will start his few days of life on earth now as a morontia being (a being between material and spiritual). The body of flesh and blood of Jesus is still lying inside the tomb of Joseph undisturbed until Gabriel and the hosts of angels dissolved the material body of Jesus instantaneously, so that there was no sign of Jesus' physical body left in the tomb. Only the linen cloth that was left intact and untouched was on the sepulcher niche.

Edgardo Samaniego

THE MATERIA BODY OF JESUS

Paper 189:2

At ten minutes past three o'clock, as the resurrected Jesus fraternized with the assembled personalities of the seven mansion worlds of Satania, the chief of archangels – the angels of the resurrection – approached Gabriel and asked for the mortal body of Jesus.

The chief of the archangels, the angels involved in the resurrection, approached Gabriel and asked for the physical body of Jesus. They intend to put the material dead body of Jesus through a process of instantaneous dissolution. This is a celestial way that they can perform. They will perform an accelerated, immediate dissolution of the flesh and blood body of Jesus. They have the approval and permission from the Most High of Edentia thru the Chief Executive Gabriel.

They performed an accelerated dissolution of the mortal body of Jesus, laid it in the sepulcher of Joseph, wrapped in a linen cloth. The physical body of Jesus was well-nigh dissolved immediately without any trace, but the linen sheet was still left without any damage. This was to avoid the slow decay of the body of Jesus so that it may cause some controversy and more confusion for the misguided humans of that time.

When all are approved, and the hosts of celestials and midwayers' personalities assembled outside the tomb, they rolled the huge circular rock in its groove that covers the entrance of the tomb. It was early Sunday morning. All the guards witnessed with full surprise and shocked that the huge stone was moving by itself without any physical forces doing the act. They all ran away from the site, the Jewish guards ran home and reported the incident to their captain, the Roman guards ran to the fortress of Antonia and reported the incident to the centurion.

The Jewish leader was bewildered by the incident, and decided to tell all the guards that they will get a sum of money if they will tell the people that the disciples had stolen the body of Jesus. The Jewish leaders also promised to defend the Roman guards from Pilate in case he finds out that the Roman guards accept bribes.

The Christian belief in the physical resurrection of Jesus was based on an empty tomb. It was indeed a fact that the tomb was empty, but this is not the real truth of the resurrection. The tomb was really empty when the first believers arrived, and this fact, associated with that of the undoubted resurrection of the Master, led to the formulation of the belief which was not true: the teaching that the material body of

Jesus was raised from the grave. Truth having to do with spiritual realities and eternal values cannot always be built up by a combination of apparent facts. Although individual facts may be materially true, it does not follow that the association of a group of facts must necessarily lead to truthful spiritual conclusions.

The tomb of Joseph was empty, not because the body of Jesus had been rehabilitated or resurrected, but because the celestial hosts had been granted their request to afford it a special and unique dissolution, a return of the "dust to dust," without the intervention of the delays of time and without the operation of the ordinary and visible processes of mortal decay and material corruption.

The mortal remains of Jesus underwent the same natural process of elemental disintegration as characterizes all human bodies on earth, except that, in point of time, the natural mode of dissolution was greatly accelerated, hastened to the point that it became well-nigh instantaneous.

These process was done to avoid the body of Jesus of Nazareth, the Master, from the slow decay and I assumed that it will only create confusion, unfounded assumptions and unnecessary superstition when they let the material body of Jesus laid on the sepulcher niche inside the tomb of Joseph. The women who love and follow Jesus will continue to embalm Jesus on a regular basis, should his body be left as is, and that will create conflict and confusion with all the people who love him and hate him.

The mistake of the Christian belief of the material resurrection is that they did not realize that there are few ways of disposing of a dead body by Jewish and the Romans during those days and age.

They dispose of a dead body by:

1) Burial pit – throw the body in the pit, but wild animals can eat and devour the dead body.

2) Burning the dead body.

3) Feeding the dead body to the wild animals.

4) Decapitation.

Should the body of Jesus have been put to any of the above kinds of disposal of the dead; there will be no physical body to resurrect.

The true evidence of the resurrection of Christ Michael are spiritual in nature, albeit this teaching is corroborated by the testimony of many mortals of the realm who met, recognized, and communed with the resurrected morontia Master. He became a part of the personal experience of around one thousand human beings before he finally took leave of Urantia (Earth), and ascended to his Father in the Isle of Paradise.

THE DISPENSATIONAL RESURRECTION

Paper 189:3

A little after half past four o'clock this Sunday morning, Gabriel summoned the archangels to his side and made ready to inaugurate the general resurrection of the termination of the Adamic dispensation on Urantia. When the vast hosts of the seraphim and the Cherubim concerned in this great event had been marshaled in proper formation, the morontia form of Christ Michael appeared before Gabriel, saying: As my Father has life in himself, so has he given it to the Son to have life in himself.

Even Jesus Christ has not fully returned to his original being as the sovereign ruler of the local universe, in his present morontia being, he still has the authority to give life and has the full power to resurrect the sleeping will creatures of the realm.

The circuit of the archangels operated for the first time from Urantia, Gabriel and the archangel hosts moved to the place of the spiritual polarity of the planet; and when Gabriel gave the signal, saying: 'By the mandate of Michael, let the dead of a Urantia dispensation rise!" Then all the survivors of the human races of Urantia who had fallen asleep since the days of Adam, and who had not already gone on to judgment, appeared in the resurrection hall of Mansonia in readiness for morontia investiture. And in an instant, the seraphim and their associates made ready to depart for mansion worlds to accompany the resurrected creatures. Every resurrected being has a seraphic guardian, who mentors, teaches, accompanies and cares for them during their ascension career in mansion worlds.

This is the third dispensational resurrection roll call, the first is during the Planetary Prince era, before the second, which is during the arrival of Adam and Eve on Urantia, and the third is during the resurrection of Jesus Christ.

Gabriel remained and stayed on Urantia with Jesus Christ while the morontia being of the Master tarried and communed for around forty days on Earth.

And this is the recital of the events of the resurrection of Jesus as viewed by those who saw them as they really occurred, free from the limitations of partial and restricted human vision and discernment. This whole divine and glorious events testify to the power, glory, love, mercy and faithfulness of the Universal Father, the Son, the Spirit and all its spiritual associates and co-ordinates of the heavenly realms.

DISCOVERY OF THE EMPTY TOMB

Paper 189:4

As we approach the time of the resurrection of Jesus on this early Sunday morning, it should be recalled that the ten apostles were sojourning at the home of Elijah and Mary Mark, where they were asleep in the upper chamber, resting on the very couches whereon they reclined during the last supper with their Master.

This Sunday morning, they were all there except Thomas. Thomas cannot stand the situation, looking at all the rest of the apostles who are overwhelmed of what had happened to their Master, and the look on the group who are consumed with fear, grief, despair made him left the place and went to the home of Simon in Bethpage, where he thought to grieve in solitude.

In Nicodemus' home, David Zebedee, Joseph of Arimatea and some of the prominent people of Jerusalem who were also the disciples and followers of Jesus. There were around fifteen to twenty women believers at the home of Joseph of Arimathea. These people are unaware of what has just transpired in the tomb and outside the tomb.

Before three o'clock in the early Sunday morning, five of the women; Mary Magdalene, Mary the mother of the Alpheus twins, Salome, the mother of the Zebedee brothers, Joanna the wife of Chuza, and Susanna the daughter of Ezra of Alexandria. After they prepared the new embalming lotions, fresh linen sheets for embalming Jesus, they remained.

It was three-thirty in the morning when the five women arrived in the empty tomb; they saw some soldiers running in panic out to the Damascus gate. The tomb of Joseph was located in his garden on the eastern side of the road and facing the east, so there will have some light to see the inside of the tomb. When they arrived in front of the tomb, they were so surprised that the tomb was open; the stone that covered the tomb was rolled on the side. They were astonished and bewildered by what they saw, but Mary Magdalene proceeded to enter the open door to the sepulcher niche. Mary saw only the folded napkin that where Jesus' head rested, he also saw the bandages that wrapped Jesus' body intact in the sepulcher niche, and the covering sheet lay at the foot of the burial niche.

When Mary Magdalene saw all this extraordinary and shocking scene of Jesus' body disappearance, she was shocked and screamed with her lungs, crying and shouting that the body of the

Master was gone. The women outside the tomb runaway, but realized what they had done, leaving Mary alone in the tomb, so they went straight back to the tomb.

When they all came back in the tomb, Mary and the rest of the women went inside the tomb to see the absence of Jesus' body in the sepulcher niche, but only the cloth and linen that covered the body of Jesus were there, untouched. They pondered the whole situation, they thought that someone might have moved the body of Jesus to another place, but when they were confused, why were the clothes and all the linen sheets that covered the body of Jesus was still there intact and untouched. How can they move the body of Jesus with the clothes and linen sheets that cover it was left intact in the sepulcher niche?

As the five women sat outside the tomb, contemplating about the whole incident noticed a stranger standing on the side of the tomb, they were startled with the strangers sudden appearance, but Mary even still shock, approach the stranger thinking that he might be the caretaker ask him if he know anything about the disappearance of the Master's body. Mary asking the stranger; where did you take our Master's body?, Tell us where we can see his body? Jesus' body, our Master was gone, tell us where we can see him? Jesus answered them; "Did not this Jesus tell you, even in Galilee, that he would die, but that he would rise again?" These words startled the women, but they were still not able to recognize Jesus as his back obstructed the dim light. As they pondered his words, Jesus spoke one word, "Mary", with a single word full of affection and a sympathetic greeting, Mary immediately recognized the voice of the Master.

Mary suddenly and with a sense of relief rushed to Jesus and knelt, saying, "My Lord and my Master!" and the rest of the women recognized the Master in glorified form, and they all knelt down before him.

These human eyes were enabled to see the morontia form of Jesus because of the special ministry of the transformers and the midwayers in association with certain of the morontia personalities who were then accompanying Jesus.

As Mary sought to embrace his feet, Jesus said: "Touch me not, Mary, for I am not as you knew me in the flesh. In this form will I tarry with you for a season before I ascend to the Father. But go, all of you, now and tell my apostles – and Peter- that I have risen, and that you have talked with me."

Normally, a morontia form is not visible to the human naked eyes, but with the authority of Christ Michael, he asked the ministry of transformers and midwayers to have his morontia form be visible to the human eyes while he tarries on earth for a while. But with this form, he cannot be touched and actually, he can go through closed doors and walls.

After they recovered from the shock of what had happened, they ran back to the city and to the home of Elijah Mark, where they told the apostles what had just happened in the tomb. Mary Magdalene told them all the words that Jesus had said. When Peter heard his name being spoken by the Master, Peter immediately started to run toward the tomb as John followed him.

PETER AND JOHN AT THE TOMB

Paper 189:5

As the two apostles raced for Golgotha and the tomb of Joseph, Peter's thoughts alternated between fear and hope; he feared to meet the Master, but his hope was aroused by the story that Jesus had sent special word to him. He was half persuaded that Jesus was really alive.

Peter was confused about the situation, whether he will believe that the Master really resurrected as the women told them. John, in the other hand, felt a sense of ecstasy, joy and hope that the Master had risen. John, as a younger and faster person than Peter, reached the tomb first. John entered the tomb and saw what was exactly Mary Magdalene told them. Peter saw the inside of the tomb, with the clothes and linen sheets intact, and both of them sat down and pondered what had really happened to their Master's remains and all they have seen. Peter thought that the enemy might have stolen the body of Jesus, but John pointed out that why have the grave clothes, linen bandages are left intact.

When they examined the sepulcher niche for the second time and went back out, they saw Mary Magdalene crying and downcast that the apostles did not believe her that he saw the Master and spoke to her. But as Mary stayed in the tomb when Peter and John left, the Master appeared again to Mary saying; "Be not doubting; have the courage to believe what you have seen and heard. Go back to my apostles and again tell them that I have risen, that I will appear to them, and that presently I will go before them into Galilee as I promised. Jesus tried to assure and strengthen Mary Magdalene's faith in his resurrection and tell his apostles again that he really have risen.

MORONTIA APPEARANCES OF JESUS

Paper 190:0

The resurrected Jesus is now prepared to spend a short period on Urantia for the purpose of experiencing the ascending morontia career of a mortal of the realms. Although this time of the morontia life is to be spent on the world of his mortal incarnation, it will, however, be in all respects the counterpart of the experience of Satania mortals who pass through the progressive morontia life of the seven mansion worlds of Jerusem.

The purpose of the Master tarrying for a while on Earth was to continue teaching about the will of the Universal Father and demonstrate to the world that to attain eternal life, one must pass through physical death and experience the transition from material to morontial, then finally to spiritual being in eternal existence.

At this age, mortal beings must pass through physical death, experiencing ascension stages while progressively transforming into a higher and higher level of spiritual status. No mortal of the realm can see the brilliance and intensity of the power of the Almighty Supreme and survive. A mortal being must pass the ascension career and 570 spiritual transformations before they become a fully spiritualized being who can stand before the divine, glorious, spiritual luminosity and brilliance of the Universal Father in the Isle of Paradise.

All this power, which is inherent in Jesus, the endowment of life and which enabled him to rise from the dead, is the very gift of eternal life which he bestows upon kingdom believers, and which even now makes certain their resurrection from the bonds of natural death.

As Jesus said, "My Father and I are one," a testimony that clarifies the true nature and attributes of the Universal Father: love, mercy, and forgiveness.

The absolute faith in the resurrection of Jesus is the foundation of the gospel teaching of Jesus Christ as the risen Messiah, the Savior and salvation of all mankind.

Mary Magdalene was the leader of the women's corps and, being so devoted to the teaching of their Master, became emboldened when she thought that the image of a man standing beside them was the caretaker of the garden. She unhesitatingly asked him about the whereabouts of the Master's body, forgetting that she was a Jewish woman.

HERALDS OF THE RESURRECTION

Paper 190:1

The apostles did not want Jesus to leave them; therefore, they had slighted all his statements about dying, along with his promises to rise again. They were not expecting the resurrection as it came, and they refused to believe until they were confronted with the compulsion of unimpeachable evidence and the absolute proof of their own experiences.

The apostles still refused to believe the five women who had actually spoken to the risen Master. Mary Magdalene returned to the tomb, and the rest of the women went back to Joseph's house and told their experience to the other women, who believed them. The daughter of Joseph of Arimathea and the four women who had seen Jesus went to the house of Nicodemus. They related the incident to Joseph, Nicodemus, David Zebedee, and the other men in the house of Nicodemus.

Nicodemus and the other men doubted the story; they suspected that the Jews had taken the body of Jesus. Joseph and David chose to believe and ran to the tomb to find out for themselves, and they saw exactly what the women had described. They were the last people to see the sepulcher as it was, with the clothes and linen bandages intact. The Jewish high priest ordered the temple guard to go to the tomb, remove all the cloth and linen, and dispose of them off the nearby cliff.

As David and Joseph saw what had happened in the tomb, they ran back to Elijah Mark's home to have a conference with the ten apostles in the upper chamber. John Zebedee believed, but Peter still had doubts, as he had not yet seen the risen Master. The rest still did not believe and thought that the Jews had taken the body of Jesus.

David did not argue with the rest of the apostles; instead, he left to go back to Nicodemus's home and organize the messengers to gather and prepare to fulfill their last mission to herald the Master's resurrection. Before leaving the confused and still doubtful apostles, David, the chief of communication and intelligence, left Judas's bag containing the apostolic funds and handed it to Matthew Levi.

At half past nine o'clock, all twenty-six messengers of David were present, and he assembled them in the spacious courtyard of Nicodemus's home. David addressed the assembly, saying:

"Men and brethren, I thank you for serving the mission of the kingdom as faithful volunteer messengers and workers. I now release you from your oaths and disband the messenger corps. The Master does not need the service of the messenger corps anymore. He told us before he was arrested that he would face death, but he would rise again on the third day. I have seen the empty tomb, except that the cloth and all linen bandages are still intact, and Mary Magdalene and the four women with her saw Jesus and talked to him. Go and tell the people that Jesus has risen from the dead."

Before ten o'clock Sunday morning, the twenty-six messengers of David were dispatched to the home of Lazarus in Bethany and to all the believer centers from Beersheba in the south to Damascus and Sidon in the north, and from Philadelphia in the east to Alexandria in the west.

David went to the home of Joseph for his mother, and they went to Bethany to join the family of Jesus. David abode there with Martha and Mary until they disposed of their earthly possessions and joined Lazarus on their journey to Philadelphia.

After a week, John Zebedee took Mary, the mother of Jesus, to his home in Bethsaida. James, Jesus's eldest brother, remained with the rest of his family in Jerusalem. Ruth remained at Bethany with Lazarus's sisters. The rest of Jesus's family returned to Galilee. David Zebedee left Bethany with Martha and Mary for Philadelphia early in June, the day after his marriage to Ruth, Jesus's youngest sister.

JESUS APPEARED AT BETHANY

Paper 190:2

From the time of the morontia resurrection until the hour of his spirit ascension on high, Jesus made nineteen separate appearances in visible form to his believers on earth. He did not appear to his enemies nor to those who could not make spiritual use of his manifestation in visible form. His first appearance was to the five women at the tomb; his second, to Mary Magdalene, also at the tomb.

Jesus carefully chose the people to whom he would appear in the morontia form. He did not want to create fear, confusion, superstition, unnecessary violence and death. He first appeared to Mary Magdalene and the four women with her. Jesus knew that Mary Magdalene's devotion and complete faith and trust in him made it appropriate to first appear to her and made his second appearance to Mary.

Jesus' third appearance was to his oldest brother James; it happened in the garden of Lazarus before the garden of the resurrected brother of Martha and Mary. James was almost fully believing in the mission of his eldest brother on earth, but he had separated himself from the mission of Jesus and made it more confusing and doubtful regarding the later claims of the apostles that Jesus was the Messiah. Mary Magdalene arrived, as did David Zebedee and his mother, together with Jude, after he talked with David and Salome.

While James stood in the garden near the empty tomb of Lazarus, he sensed and felt someone behind him, and he felt someone touch his shoulder. When he looked behind, he saw this strange form that shocked and startled him so much that he could not move. Then the strange form spoke: "I came to call you to the service of the kingdom. Join your brethren and follow and preach the service of the kingdom." Although Jesus' morontia form was hard to recognize, his voice with its most distinctive, sympathetic, and loving tone could be easily recognized as the voice of the Master himself.

James, believing that it was really Jesus with him but in a strange form, started to fall on his knees, exclaiming, "My Father, my Brother," but Jesus bade him to stand up, and they walked around the garden and talked for a few minutes, discussing past experiences and the coming future ahead. As they walked near the house, Jesus said, "Farewell, James, until I greet you all together."

James rushed to the house, even while they were looking for him at Bethpage, exclaiming: "I have seen Jesus and talked with him, visited with him. He is not dead; he has risen! Jesus vanished before me, saying farewell to see you again." Jude had just arrived, and James retold his experience with Jesus. James announced that he would not return to Galilee, and David exclaimed, "Women have seen him, and strong-hearted men begin to see him too. I am also excited to see him for myself."

David did not wait long for the next appearance of Jesus. Before two o'clock that afternoon, in the home of Martha and Mary, Jesus appeared for the fourth time to his friends and family, about twenty people. The Master stood in the open back door and said, "Peace be upon you. Greetings to those once near me in the flesh and fellowship with my brothers and sisters in the kingdom of heaven."

AT THE HOME OF JOSEPH

Paper 190:3

The fifth morontia appearance of Jesus to the recognition of mortal eyes occurred in the presence of some twenty-five women believers assembled at the home of Joseph of Arimathea, at about fifteen minutes past four o'clock on the same Sunday afternoon.

Mary Magdalene had just returned to Joseph's house before Jesus appeared. James (Jesus' brother) wanted that the apostles should not to be told of the appearance of Jesus in Bethany. While Mary was telling the women to keep the occurrences secret, still in a state of excitement, a solemn, glorious, and gentle hush came over them. Jesus greeted them: "Peace be upon you." Jesus said, in the fellowship of the kingdom, there shall be neither Jew nor Gentile, rich nor poor, free nor bond, man nor woman. "You also are called to publish the good news of the liberty of mankind through the gospel of sonship with God in the kingdom of heaven. Go and tell the world about the Fatherhood of God and the brotherhood/sisterhood of mankind." Jesus told them, "I will always be with you everywhere you are in this world."

This appearance was the fourth time for Mary Magdalene to witness. The news of Jesus' resurrection leaked to the Jews due to the messengers spreading the news to the believers, and it began to spread unintentionally until it reached the Sanhedrin. The Sanhedrists were greatly incited by the rumor. After a discussion with Annas, Caiaphas called a meeting at 8 o'clock that night. They were all panicky and confused about what was happening. They suggested that anyone who talked about Jesus' resurrection should be thrown out of the synagogues, or even proposed that anyone saying such a thing be put to death. But their meeting broke up in chaos and confusion. They had no idea that their trouble was just beginning regarding the risen Master.

APPEARANCE TO THE GREEK

Paper 190:4

About half past four o'clock at the home of Flavius, the Master made his sixth appearance to some forty Greek believers there assembled. While they were engaged in discussing the reports of the Master's resurrection, he manifested himself in their midst, notwithstanding that the doors were securely fastened, and, speaking to them, said: "Peace be upon you."

Jesus said, "While the Son of Man appeared on earth among the Jews, he came to minister and make a connection with everyone, whether Jews, Gentiles, or any race. Everyone is a child of God; therefore, go and spread the truth of the gospel of the kingdom." And Jesus disappeared again. The Greeks were so awed and still in a state of fear that they remained inside.

Jesus was thinking about his apostles, but still, he wished to give them more time to contemplate and reflect on the whole affair.

The Sanhedrists had to face these problems, which were becoming unmanageable for them.

THE WALK WITH TWO BROTHERS

Paper 190:5

At Emmaus, about seven miles west of Jerusalem, there lived two brothers shepherds who had spent the Passover week in Jerusalem attending the sacrifices, ceremonials, and feasts. Cleopas, the elder, was a partial believer in Jesus; at least he had been cast out of the synagogue. His brother Jacob was not a believer, although he was much intrigued by what he had heard about the Master's teaching and works.

Before five o'clock this Sunday afternoon, around three miles outside Jerusalem, there were two brothers walking along the road to Emmaus, talking about Jesus and his teachings and works. They also talked about the rumor of Jesus' resurrection that the women found his tomb empty and Jesus talked with them. Cleopas partially believed the news, but Jacob thought that the whole story was a lie and a fraud.

While they continued to walk and argue about Jesus, the morontia form of Jesus appeared to them for the seventh time. Though Cleopas had often heard Jesus teach and had eaten with the Master on several occasions at the home of a Jerusalem believer, he did not recognize the Master even when Jesus started to talk to them.

As they continued to walk, Jesus politely asked what words they were talking about. With sadness on the face of Cleopas, he said: "Can it be that you sojourn in Jerusalem and know not the things which have recently happened?" The Master asked, "What things?" and Cleopas replied: "If you do not know about these matters, you are the only one in Jerusalem who has not heard these rumors concerning Jesus of Nazareth, who was a prophet mighty in words and deeds before God and all the people. The chief priests and our rulers delivered him up to the Romans and demanded that they crucify him. Many of us hoped that he was the one who would deliver Israel from the bondage of the Gentiles. He was crucified and died, but it has been three days now since he was crucified, and some of the women believers went to his tomb very early today, and they found the tomb empty. But they said they saw him and talked to Jesus."

And when these women told some of their men friends, two men went to the tomb, and they found the tomb empty. Jacob interrupted his brother and said, "But they did not see Jesus." As they continued to walk and talk, Jesus said to them: "How slow you are to comprehend the truth! When you tell me that it is about the teaching and work of this man that you are talking about, may I enlighten you, since I am more familiar with his teaching. Do you not remember that this Jesus always taught that his kingdom is not of this world? That all men are created equal in the Fatherhood of the Kingdom and the Brotherhood of mankind? That the power and glory of the Almighty Father will be upon all who believe, have faith, and trust the Lord? That all who fully believe in him shall have salvation and eternal life?"

As they approached the village near their home, they invited Jesus to dine with them, as it was already late in the night. Jesus accepted their invitation and sat to dine with the brothers. The brothers gave him the bread to bless, and as Jesus started to break the bread and was about to say a prayer, Cleopas finally recognized Jesus, "It is the Master!" Then the Master instantly disappeared.

The brothers realized the reason why they had felt a burning feeling of being overcome by his glory and power as Jesus spoke while walking with them. They rushed from the house to Jerusalem and spread the good news. They ran to where the apostles were in the upper chamber of Mary Mark's house and told them that the Master was with them until he broke the bread in their home and vanished.

APPEARANCES TO THE APOSTLES
AND OTHER LEADERS

Paper 191:0

RESURRECTION Sunday was a terrible day in the lives of the apostles; ten of them spent the larger part of the day in the upper chamber behind barred doors. They might have fled from Jerusalem, but they were afraid of being arrested by the agents of the Sanhedrin if they were found abroad. Thomas was brooding over his troubles alone at Bethpage. He would have fared better had he remained with his fellow apostles, and he would have aided them in directing their discussions along more helpful lines.

The ten apostles were still in a state of confusion and fear; they did not really know the truth of what was transpiring outside the news that the Master had resurrected. But John upheld the idea that Jesus really had risen. He remembered Jesus telling them at least five times that He would die but would rise again on the third day. John could influence his brother James and Nathaniel, but because he was the youngest of the apostles, they did not really take him seriously.

The apostles received information from John Mark. He got information from the temple and the people around who heard rumors of Jesus' resurrection, but he did not think of talking to the people who had already seen the risen Jesus. This information would have been available to them if only the messengers were still with them.

Peter continued to digest all the scenes he had witnessed at the empty tomb that the grave clothes were still intact, as though Jesus' body had simply evaporated. Peter was racking his brain as to why Jesus appeared to the women and not to the apostles. Maybe the Master did not want to appear to them because Peter had denied Him three times. But it also gave Peter hope when he recalled what the women had said that the Master instructed them, "Go tell my apostles and Peter." Peter was still in a state of doubt and faith. At about eight o'clock, he decided to venture outside the courtyard to get away from the rest of the apostles. He thought that Jesus might appear to them if he were not there, perhaps as a consequence of his denial of the Master.

James Zebedee had at first advocated that they all go to the tomb. He vigorously insisted that they should go to the tomb to get to the bottom of the mystery. It was Nathaniel who reminded them of what their Master had told them before to avoid putting themselves in danger or possibly death. James conformed and chose to wait patiently with the others. He was disappointed that Jesus had not yet appeared to them. James and the apostles had no knowledge of Jesus' appearance to other groups and individuals.

Andrew mostly listened and simply observed the situation. He also had doubts about everything that was happening, but he enjoyed his freedom from the responsibility of leadership since the Master had released him from it.

Nathaniel helped the rest of the apostles to hold on with his positive and sustaining character, which influenced them to believe that the Master would indeed fulfill His promise to rise again on the third day.

But Simon Zelotes was so downcast and disappointed that he kept to himself, facing the wall, having lost all hope in Jesus' promise regarding the kingdom. Even the astounding news of Jesus' resurrection gave him no comfort.

Philip usually did not express himself, but this time he was very curious to know the details of Jesus' resurrection. He wanted to know if Jesus' resurrected body still bore all the scars, bruises, and fatal wounds from the crucifixion. Peter was irritated by Philip's questions, but most of the apostles were also curious to know whether the Master's resurrected body still bore those marks.

Although Matthew was confused by all the events, his main concern was about the apostolic finances. With Judas gone and David having turned over financial responsibility to him, Matthew had already seen the Master face to face before sharing his own thoughts about Jesus' resurrection.

The Alpheus twins believed their mother's statement that she had seen and spoken with the resurrected Master. Even though they did not fully understand the process of resurrection, they trusted and believed what their mother had told them.

Thomas chose to be alone, walking on the hillside, consumed by depression and confusion. He kept himself away from the rest.

The Master delayed His first appearance to the apostles for several reasons. First, He wanted them to have time to realize and remember what He had told them before His crucifixion, that He would be killed but would rise again on the third day. Jesus wanted Peter to fully understand everything about how he had behaved, acted, and reacted to the whole situation. The Master also wanted Thomas to be with them when He appeared to the group. John Mark located Thomas at the home of Simon in Bethpage early that Sunday morning and informed the rest of the apostles around eleven o'clock. If Nathaniel or any of the apostles had gone to bring Thomas back, he would have agreed to return, but he was too proud or embarrassed to come back with them. That is why it took almost a week for him to return. In the end, Peter and John went over to Bethpage and brought Thomas back with them. They wanted to go to Galilee with everyone together.

THE APPEARANCE TO PETER

Paper 191:1

It was approaching half past eight o'clock on Sunday evening when Jesus appeared to Peter the eighth morontia appearance. Peter was heavily burdened with guilt over his three denials of the Master and feared that he might be likened to Judas. He thought that perhaps he could no longer be regarded as one of Jesus' apostles. He also believed the Master might appear to the apostles only if he were not present.

While Peter was alone in the garden, deep in contemplation, the morontia Jesus appeared before him, just as Peter was imagining the face of his Master and recalling what Mary Magdalene had told him about Jesus' message: "Go tell my apostles and Peter." Clenching his fists, he said aloud, "Now I believe He is risen, and I will tell my brethren." Then suddenly, a strange form of a man appeared before him and said, "Peter, the enemy wanted to get you, but I will not let them. I know it was not from your heart that you denied me, and I forgive you even before you asked for it. Be not concerned with what you receive from the kingdom, but rather give your full devotion in service to the spiritually deprived beings on earth."

Peter and the Master walked together in the garden, talking about the past, the present, and the future. Then the Master said, "Farewell, Peter, until I see you again with your brethren." The Master disappeared from Peter's sight.

Peter was so excited by the incident that he ran inside to tell the others that the Master had appeared to him and told him to continue preaching the gospel of the kingdom. But his brother Andrew immediately dismissed his claim and told the others that Peter might just be imagining things, reminding them that Peter had once claimed to see the Master walking on the water at the Sea of Galilee.

Simon Peter was deeply hurt by Andrew's insinuation, but the Alpheus twins comforted him. They assured him they believed his testimony, just as they believed their mother, who had also seen the Master.

THE FIRST APPEARANCE TO THE APOSTLES

Paper 191:2

Shortly after nine o'clock that evening, following the departure of Cleopas and Jacob, while the Alpheus twins comforted Peter, and while Nathaniel remonstrated with Andrew, the ten apostles were assembled in the upper chamber with all the doors bolted for fear of arrest. Then, the Master, in morontia form, suddenly appeared in their midst, saying: "Peace be upon you."

Jesus asked the apostles why they were frightened, as if they had seen a ghost. He reminded them how many times He had told them, even before His arrest, that these things would happen: that one of them would betray Him, that He would be arrested at the instruction of the chief priests, and delivered up to die by crucifixion. But, as He had told them, on the third day He would rise again.

"Now," He said, "doubt no more of my resurrection, as the women, Cleopas, Jacob, and Peter have already told you. Now that you certainly know I have risen and you finally see me, go and tell the people of Galilee. Have complete faith in God the Father, in one another, and enter into the new service of the kingdom of heaven. I will tarry in Jerusalem with you for a time, until you are ready to go into Galilee. Peace be with you all."

When Jesus finished speaking, He instantly vanished from their sight. They all fell on their faces and began to worship and venerate their risen Master.

WITH THE MORONTIA CREATURES

Paper 191:3

The next day, Monday, was spent wholly with the morontia creatures then present on Urantia. As participants in the Master's morontia-transition experience, there had come to Urantia more than one million morontia directors and associates, together with transition mortals of various orders from the seven mansion worlds of Satania.

Jesus, being in a morontia form, sojourned with these splendid and beautiful intelligences for forty days while still on earth. The human mortals, during their ascension career, will also experience this morontia progression.

At midnight of this Monday, the morontia form of the Master was adjusted to the second stage of progression. When the Master next appears to his apostles and to the rest of his mortal children, it will be his second stage of morontia being. And as he progresses to the next stages, he will be more and more difficult to recognize.

Jesus made the transit to the third stage of morontia on Friday, April 14; to the fourth stage on Monday, the 17th; to the fifth stage on Saturday, the 22nd; to the sixth stage on Thursday, the 27th; to the seventh stage on Tuesday, May 2; to Jerusem citizenship on Sunday, the 7th; and he entered the embrace of the Most Highs of Edentia on Sunday, the 14th.

Jesus does experience the ascension career, as all the mortals of the realm will experience during their morontia life after material death. The ascendant beings will progressively traverse the seven spheres of heaven while, in conjunction, experiencing several progressive spiritual transformations from mansion worlds, to Jerusem, to Edentia, to Salvington, to Uversa, to Havona, and finally to the Isle of Paradise, the dwelling place of the Universal Father and all His sons, all His spiritual associates and coordinates. Jesus finished and fully completed his seventh and final bestowal, becoming the sovereign and absolute ruler of the local universe of Nebadon, which he created.

THE TENTH APPEARANCE (AT PHILADELPHIA)

Paper 191:4

The tenth morontia manifestation of Jesus to mortal recognition occurred a short time after eight o'clock on Tuesday, April 11, at Philadelphia, where he showed himself to Abner and Lazarus and some one hundred and fifty of their associates, including more than fifty of the evangelistic corps of seventy.

This tenth appearance of Jesus to more people at one time made his resurrection more tangible and concrete to the people. Jesus' morontia form appeared before the people after the opening of the special meeting in the synagogue organized by Abner to discuss the crucifixion of Jesus and the news of his resurrection brought by David's messengers.

Lazarus, who was resurrected from his supposed death, was a member and present at the meeting. Some people witnessed and heard of Lazarus' resurrection, although Jesus told the people that Lazarus was not completely dead when he brought him back to life.

When the meeting inside the synagogue was just about to start, presided over by Abner and with Lazarus standing in the pulpit, the morontia form of the Master appeared before the audience, standing between Abner and Lazarus.

Jesus greeted the congregation: "Peace be with you. We all know that we only have one Father in heaven and one gospel of the kingdom. The truth of the gift of eternal life is to those who believe and have the unswerving faith in the Universal Father's love and mercy for all. I proclaim and declare to you the love and service of the Father in Paradise, as I love and serve you and also give that love and service to your fellow human beings."

Jesus continued to tell the congregation to spread the will of the Universal Father the "Fatherhood of God and the Brotherhood of Mankind" to all: to the Jews, Gentiles, Greeks, Romans, Persians, Ethiopians, and to the rest of the world. "Soon I will send the Spirit of Truth that will dwell upon all in this world."

When Jesus finished his admonitions, he said, "My peace I leave with you," and then he vanished from their sight. This congregation was one of the largest crowds of people assembled who saw the resurrected Jesus, second only to the five hundred people who saw him in Galilee.

The next morning, these apostles who saw the Master began to tell the people that they had seen the risen Master. The next day, Wednesday, Jesus spent his time with the morontia associates without interruption, and with some delegates from the mansion worlds and from throughout the local system of the constellation of Norlatiadek. They all rejoiced, knowing that the Creator himself is one of the same order of intelligence as they are.

SECOND APPEARANCE TO THE APOSTLES

Paper 191:5

Thomas spent a lonesome week alone with himself in the hills around Olivet. During this time, he saw only those at Simon's house and John Mark. It was about nine o'clock on Saturday, April 15, when the two apostles found him back with them at their rendezvous at the Mark home.

The following day, Thomas listened to the stories of the Master's resurrection from the dead, the various stories about the resurrection and appearances that he listened to. But after all those testimonies, he still refused to believe. He thought that Peter's testimony of seeing the resurrected Master was only an illusion and that he was trying to make them believe. Nathaniel also failed to convince him. Thomas was beginning to enjoy the attention he was getting, as he had been away for almost a week. He was getting unconscious pleasure from all the attention and time that the other apostles were giving to him.

They were having their evening meal after six o'clock. Peter was sitting beside Thomas, and Nathaniel was sitting on the other side of Thomas. Thomas said, "I will not believe until I see the Master with my own eyes and touch with my finger the mark of the nail on the Master's hands." As they ate while the doors were securely closed, the morontia form of the Master appeared before them, standing directly in front of Thomas inside the curvature of the table, and said, "Peace be upon you. For a full week have I tarried that all of you may see me together. As my Father sent me to the world to preach the gospel of the kingdom, so send I you to the whole world to preach the gospel of the kingdom of the Father.

You are about to reveal to the whole world the truth, the living and loving truth of the Universal Father towards the whole universe and universes. Let the love, mercy, faith, and devotion of the omnipotent, omniscient, and omnipresent Father destroy ignorance, backward tradition, prejudice, and hate.

The Jews have extolled goodness, the Greeks have exalted beauty; the Hindus preach devotion, the faraway ascetics teach reverence; the Romans demand loyalty; but I require of my disciples life, a life of loving service to your fellow brethren in the flesh."

And as he continued to talk, he looked at Thomas and said, "And you, Thomas, who said you would not believe unless you could see me and put your finger in the nail marks on my hand, have now beheld me and heard my words; and though you see no nail marks on my hands, since I am raised in this form a morontia form that one day when you leave the world, you will all become like this kind of form. Now, Thomas, I know you will believe, and all the doubts in your heart will disappear." When Thomas heard those words directly from the risen Master, he fell on his knees and exclaimed, "My Lord and my Master!" And then Jesus said to Thomas, "You have believed, Thomas, because you have seen me and heard me speak. Blessed are those who believe in me even though they did not see and hear me with their mortal eyes and ears." Then Jesus vanished from their sight after speaking those words.

The eleven apostles were now completely convinced of the Master's resurrection, and they had full confidence to proclaim the good news of the risen Jesus. Early the next morning, they started out on their journey to Galilee to spread the news of the risen Master.

THE ALEXANDRIAN APPEARANCE

Paper 191:6

While the eleven apostles were on their way to Galilee, drawing near the end of their journey on Tuesday evening, April 18, at about half past eight o'clock, Jesus appeared to Rodan and eighty other believers in Alexandria. This was the Master's twelfth appearance in morontia form. Jesus appeared before these Greeks and Jews at the conclusion of the report delivered by David's messenger regarding the crucifixion.

The messenger, Nathan of Busiris, who served the Jerusalem–Alexandria route, conveyed the news that Jesus had been crucified and had died. Nathan told the Alexandrians that David sent the word saying, "The Master will be crucified and die, but he will rise again on the third day."

While Nathan was speaking, the morontia form of Jesus appeared in full view of all the people present. Jesus said:

"Peace be upon you. My Father sent me to the world to declare and preach the kingdom of God, which is for the whole world and not just for one race of people, or a particular nation or group of people. The gospel of the kingdom belongs to Jews, Gentiles, and all races and beliefs to male and female, poor and rich, every human being on earth. You will love and serve mankind as I love and serve you. Go you, therefore, into the entire world preaching this gospel, and lo, I will always be with you, even to the end of the world.

Jesus freely submitted to death, demonstrating that death is the way to eternal life. He died on Friday afternoon, and then he rose again in the very early hours of Sunday morning in morontia form the form that will ascend in progression from the mansion worlds right up to the Isle of Paradise. These ascending experiences will also be experienced by all of us mortal beings on earth, and by the other mortal beings of the evolutionary worlds who will undergo the ascension career from material death to morontia existence and finally to spiritual life in eternity.

THE APPEARANCES IN GALILEE

Paper 192:0

By the time the apostles left Jerusalem for Galilee, the Jewish leaders had quieted down considerably. Since Jesus appeared only to his family of kingdom believers, and since the apostles were in hiding and did no public preaching, the rulers of the Jews concluded that the gospel movement was, after all, effectively crushed.

The Jewish priests and leaders thought that Jesus' movement was finished and dismantled. They could not see any action or movement from Jesus' apostles and followers.

That week, the apostles tarried in Jerusalem, and Mary, the mother of Jesus, was with the women believers in Joseph of Arimathea's home, together waiting for the next development regarding the fact that Jesus had risen. They could only wait for what might happen at any moment.

The apostles stopped a few times on their way to Galilee to share the story of the risen Master. That is why they arrived in Bethsaida late that Wednesday night. The next day, Thursday, they woke up late, almost at noon, for their breakfast. That day, they simply spent their time together talking about the whole situation.

APPEARANCE BY THE LAKE

Paper 192:1

About six o'clock Friday morning, April 21, the morontia Master made his thirteenth appearance, the first in Galilee, to the ten apostles as their boat drew near the shore close to the usual landing place at Bethsaida.

Simon Peter suggested that they go fishing after the apostles spent the afternoon and early evening on Thursday in Zebedee's home. They all tried to catch some fish with no luck all night long, but it did not disappoint them, as they were consumed by the greater incident of the risen Master. When daylight appeared, they decided to go back to Bethsaida. As they neared the shoreline of the beach, they saw someone by the boat shed standing beside a fire. They thought it was John Mark coming to welcome them with the catch, but as they came nearer, they saw it was the Master. They wondered why the Master would appear to them out in the open and in nature. Jesus had earlier told them that he would meet them in Galilee.

As they dropped the anchor of the big boat and were about to enter the small boat, Jesus yelled, "Lads, have you caught anything?" and when they answered, "No," he spoke again: "Cast the net on the right side of the boat, and you will catch some fish." Although they were not really sure who the man was, they cast the net on the right side of the boat. They did not wait long, as the net was filled with fish. John Zebedee was quick to perceive that the man who told them to cast the net on the right side of the boat was no other than the Master himself, and John whispered it to Peter, "It is the Master."

John Mark was up and present on the shore, seeing the apostles coming from the boat with the net full of fish. When he ran down to greet them, he saw eleven men, but one was unrecognized, and he surmised that it must be the Master. And it was truly Jesus in morontia form. John rushed and knelt and said to Jesus, "My Lord and my Master." Jesus spoke to John, "Well, John, I am glad to see you again and in carefree Galilee, where we can have a good visit. Stay with us, John, and have breakfast."

All the apostles were astonished and forgot to bring the fish with them. Jesus spoke, "Bring in your fish, as we have the fire ready, and we have plenty of bread to share for breakfast."

While John paid respect to the Master, Peter was mesmerized by the image of the fire, as he reminisced about the midnight fire in Annas's courtyard, where he had disowned the Master. Then Peter shook his head and knelt at the Master's feet, saying, "My Lord and my Master!"

The apostles hauled in the net, counted the fish, and there were 153 large ones. It was not a miracle in the way they caught the fish; they merely cast the net in the right spot, and the Master just knew that the fish would be in that spot.

John Mark brought seven good-sized fish, and Jesus put them on the fire. When the fish were ready, the Master invited them to sit: "Come now, all of you, to have breakfast with me." Jesus broke some bread and then gave it to John to serve the rest of the apostles, together with the fish. When John finished giving all the apostles fish and bread, Jesus asked him to sit down, and the Master served John bread and fish. As all the apostles ate, Jesus recounted all their experiences.

This was the third time Jesus manifested himself to the group. The apostles did not immediately recognize Jesus' appearance on the shore because there were some fish merchants around, and the apostles might have thought that the person who asked if they had caught any fish was one of the fish merchants.

Jesus spent one hour with the apostles on the beach and walked with them two by two after eating. All eleven apostles had come down from Jerusalem. Simon Zelotes grew weary and despondent as they neared Galilee, so when they reached Bethsaida, he went back to his home. Before Jesus departed, he directed that two of the apostles should volunteer to go to Simon Zelotes. Peter and Andrew immediately volunteered.

VISITING WITH THE APOSTLES TWO AND TWO

Paper 192:2

When they had finished breakfast, and while the others sat by the fire, Jesus beckoned to Peter and to John that they should come with him for a stroll on the beach. As they walked along, Jesus said to John, "John, do you love me?" And when John answered, "Yes, Master, with all my heart," the Master said: "Then, John, give up your intolerance and learn to love men as I have loved you.

Jesus continued by saying to devote your life to proving that love is the greatest thing in the world. It is the divine love of God that beckons men to seek salvation and the eternal. Love is the ancestor and source of spiritual goodness, the essence of truth and beauty. These are the foundation of Jesus' teaching: love, and the Universal Father is the origin and source of eternal love.

Jesus then turned to Peter and asked, "Peter, do you love me?" Peter answered, "Lord, you know I love you with all my soul." Then said Jesus: "If you love me, Peter, feed my lambs. Minister to the weak, the poor, the young, and the destitute. Preach without hesitation and fear; treat everyone with the same love as the Father loves everyone. The Universal Father is no respecter of persons. Serve and forgive your fellow men as I have served and forgiven you. Let the experience of life teach you the value of meditation and the power of intelligent reflection."

After they had walked along farther, Jesus asked Peter, "Peter, do you really love me?" And Simon Peter answered, "Yes, Lord, you know that I love you." And again said Jesus: "Then take good care of my sheep. Be a good and true shepherd to the flock. Be always sincere and honest with your brethren. Be aware of your enemy, and be on alert and on guard at all times. Look out and pray."

After a few meters farther, Jesus asked Peter again for the third time, "Peter, do you truly love me?" And then Peter, feeling slightly saddened by the Master's seeming distrust of him, said with strong feeling, "Lord, you know all things, and therefore you know that I really and truly love you." Then Jesus said, "Feed my sheep. Do not forsake the flock. Be an example and inspiration to all of your fellow shepherds. Devote yourself to the welfare of others, as I have devoted my life to your welfare and the world. Always follow after me, even to the end."

Peter took the last statement of Jesus literally, that he should continue to follow Jesus everywhere. Peter turned to Jesus and pointed at John, "If I follow after you, what does this man do?" Jesus, perceiving that Peter had misunderstood his words, said, "Peter, be not concerned about what your brethren shall be doing. Do not worry about what the other will be doing. Just make sure that you follow me."

When they returned to the rest of the apostles, Jesus went with Andrew and James to walk and talk. While they were walking for a few minutes, Jesus asked Andrew, "Andrew, do you trust me?" And when Andrew heard Jesus ask such a question, he stopped and stood still and answered with a sound of assurance, "Yes, Master, I trust you, and you well know that I do." Then Jesus said, "Andrew, if you trust me, trust your brethren more – even Peter. I once trusted you with the leadership of your brethren. You must trust each other, as I will leave you all and go to my Father. When the time comes that your brethren will be scattered and separated from each other because of persecution, look after John, my brother in the flesh. He is young and inexperienced in life. Go and continue to trust me, for I will be with you and not fail you. When you are finished here on earth, you shall come and be with me in Paradise."

Then Jesus turned to James, asking, "James, do you trust me?" And James replied, "Yes, Master, I trust you with all my heart." Then Jesus said, "James, if you trust me more, you will be more patient with your brethren. If you always trust me, you will be better and affectionate with all the believers. Always remember that what you sow, you will reap. Always pray for peace and harmony. The spirit of living faith will sustain you and give you strength when the time comes for you to drink the cup of sacrifice. But do not be afraid. When your time has come, you will also be with me in Paradise."

Jesus talked to Thomas and Nathaniel. Jesus asked Thomas first, "Thomas, do you serve me?" Thomas replied, "Yes, Lord, I serve you now and I will serve you always." Then Jesus replied, "Thomas, if you would serve me, serve all our brethren in the flesh, even as I have served you. Always persevere and be not weary, for you are ordained by God in this service. Thomas, you must cease doubting; grow in faith and in the knowledge and wisdom of truth. Believe in God like a child, but do not act childish. Be courageous and have strong faith in God. When you finish your service here on earth, you will come with me in heaven."

Then the Master turned to Nathaniel, "Nathaniel, do you serve me?" And Nathaniel answered, "Yes, Master, and with undivided affection." Then Jesus said, "If therefore you really serve me with all your heart, also devote your service and devotion to the welfare of all your brethren in this world without reservation. Combine love with your philosophy in life and always be faithful to the Father in heaven. Do not be critical and be more understanding with your fellows. This will deliver you from disappointment and frustration. You will be with me when your work is over in this world."

The Master then talked to Matthew and Philip. He said to Philip, "Philip, do you obey me?" Then Philip answered, "Yes, Lord, I will obey you even with my life." Then said Jesus, "If you would obey me, go then to the Gentiles' land and proclaim the gospel of the kingdom. The prophets have told you that to obey is better than to sacrifice. Be faithful to the teaching of the kingdom, be courageous, and be proud to preach the teaching of the Lord. Spread the good news of eternal life to those who are living in darkness and are hungry for truth and light. Philip, free yourself from the worry of money and material goods. You will be with me when your work on this temporal world is finished."

Then the Master turned to Matthew, "Matthew, do you have in your heart to obey me?" Matthew replied, "Yes, Lord, I am fully dedicated to do your will." Then Jesus said to Matthew, "Matthew, if you would really obey me, go forth to the world and preach the kingdom of heaven. You will no longer deal with material things but instead devote yourself to spiritual life and salvation to attain eternal life. Preach to the entire world, to all the people of the world, no matter what race they belong to. You will be with me in heaven when you have done your work on earth."

Then Jesus walked and talked with the Alpheus twins, James and Judas. Speaking to the twins, he asked, "James and Judas, do you believe in me?" And they both replied, "Yes, Master, we do believe in you." Jesus told the twins, "I will soon leave you. You can see that I have already left you in the flesh, and I will tarry here for a while in this form before I go to my Father in heaven. You always believed in me as my apostles. As my apostles, continue believing in me and in the gospel of the kingdom. Keep your faith in the Father strong and unwavering. Devote your life to the sacred teaching of the divine kingdom and preach it to the world. My Father and I have a far better world for you waiting when the time comes for you to ascend on high."

Jesus returned at almost ten o'clock from the Alpheus twins' visit and said to the rest of the apostles, "Farewell, until I meet you all on the mount of your ordination tomorrow at noontime." When he finished talking, he vanished from their sight.

.

ON THE MOUNT OF ORDINATION

Paper 192:3

At noon on Saturday, April 22, the eleven apostles assembled by appointment on the hill near Capernaum, and Jesus appeared among them. This meeting occurred on the very mount where the Master had set them apart as his apostles and as ambassadors of the Father's kingdom on earth. This was the Father's fourteenth morontia manifestation.

As the eleven apostles waited, kneeling in a circle on the amount the very same amount of their ordination as ambassadors of the kingdom they were reminded of their consecration to the service of the Father's kingdom.

This time, the way the Master spoke was more divine and powerful. He spoke with the tone of complete authority and power over the whole universe. The Master assured the apostles of his complete love and support in their work in the world, which would surely encounter challenges, struggle, rejection, even death for some of them. After the Master re-dedicated the apostles to the work of the kingdom, he vanished after bidding them farewell.

Jesus did not appear to anyone for a full week. The apostles were left wondering and felt lost, believing the Master had gone for good. They did not know what was truly happening; they thought the Master had already ascended to the Father. So, they remained in Bethsaida for a while.

In reality, during this entire week, Jesus spent his time with the morontia creatures on earth, dealing with the affairs and processes of the morontia transition period, which he was presently undergoing. Jesus could only commune and communicate with the morontia beings concerning his coming ascension.

THE LAKESIDE GATHERING

Paper 192:4

Word of the appearances of Jesus was spreading throughout Galilee, and every day increasing numbers of believers arrived at the Zebedee home to inquire about the Master's resurrection and to find out the truth about these reputed appearances.

More and more people knew the news of the resurrection and the appearance of Jesus, as the people who saw him spread the news all over the towns. The believers went to Zebedee's home to find the full details of Jesus' resurrection and appearances. Peter sent out word early in the week that there would be a public meeting held by the seaside the next Sabbath at three o'clock in the afternoon.

On that Sabbath day, Saturday, April 29th, at three o'clock in the afternoon, more than five hundred believers from the surrounding Capernaum gathered at Bethsaida to listen to Peter make his first preach after the resurrection of Jesus. Peter gave a convincing testimony regarding Jesus' resurrection, and most of the believers who were there believed in the resurrection and appearance of Jesus.

Peter concluded his sermon by affirming the resurrection and appearance of Jesus by saying, "We assert that Jesus is not dead, that he has risen from the tomb; we proclaim and testify that we saw him and talked with him." As he finished talking, the morontia form of Jesus appeared beside him in front of the congregation, and Jesus said, "Peace be upon you, and my peace I leave with you." After Jesus said these words, a familiar greeting from him, he vanished instantly. This was the fifteenth appearance of Jesus in morontia form. More and more people witnessed the appearance of Jesus in morontia form, and more and more people believed in his resurrection.

The apostles reckoned that the words of the Master when they were on the mount of ordination indicated that the Master would make an appearance to the group of Galilean believers, and that after that, they would return to Jerusalem. Early Sunday morning, April 30th, the eleven apostles left Bethsaida for Jerusalem. On their way to Jerusalem, they performed several teachings in the Jordan area, which is why they only arrived at Mark's home on the 3rd of May, later that afternoon.

Sadly, before they reached the home of John Mark, they heard the news that Elijah Mark had died of a brain hemorrhage. John Mark comforted and assured his mother, while the rest of the apostles shared their sympathy with the family. John Mark warmly told his brethren that they could continue to stay in the upper chamber of their house. The apostles made this upper chamber of John Mark's home their headquarters until the Pentecost had finished.

The apostles made sure that their movements would not be noticed by the Jewish authorities by going out at night time with absolute discretion. They did not even come to the funeral of Elijah Mark. They just remained secluded in the upper chamber.

On Thursday night in the upper chamber of John Mark's home, the apostles decided to start the public teaching of the new gospel of the risen Lord, with the exception of Thomas, Simon Zelotes, and the Alpheus twins. They were already changing the essence of the preaching from the Fatherhood of God and the Brotherhood of Man to the proclamation of the resurrection of Jesus. Nathaniel opposed this concept of teaching, but he could not win against the influence of Peter and the strong enthusiasm of the rest of the apostles and women believers.

This is the reason why the true essence of the Master's teaching of the Fatherhood of God and the Brotherhood of Mankind was changed by Peter and the rest of the apostles. They changed the religion of Jesus to the religion about Jesus.

This can be confusing to many believers. A good example of this kind of faith is Buddhism, founded by Siddhartha Gautama in the 5th century, teaching about spirituality. And the people ended up worshipping him instead of simply learning about his teaching.

Jesus was the messenger of God the Father. That is why Jesus repeatedly preached to the people to believe in and worship the Universal Father. Jesus is the way to the Father; he manifested the Father's attributes, nature, and will.

FINAL APPEARANCES AND ASCENSION

Paper 193:0

The sixteenth morontia manifestation of Jesus occurred on Friday, May 5, in the courtyard of Nicodemus, about nine o'clock at night. On this evening, the Jerusalem believers had made their first attempt to get together since the resurrection. Assembled here at this time were the eleven apostles, the women's corps and their associates, and about fifty leading disciples of the Master, including a number of Greeks. This company of believers had been visiting informally for more than half an hour when, suddenly, the morontia Master appeared in full view and immediately began to instruct them. Jesus said:

In this gathering, all the apostles are present, with the women's corps and their group of associates. There are also present fifty leading disciples of Jesus, and some Greek believers. This group of believers is in the courtyard of Nicodemus' home discussing the past few days that are full of extraordinary occurrences: the crucifixion, death, and now the resurrection of the Master. They are all sharing their experiences and opinions about the risen Master, when suddenly, the morontia form of the Master appeared in full view to all the people in the courtyard. Then Jesus said:

"Peace be upon you." The Master then continued to talk, acknowledging that he is present with the top leaders and leading associates of men and women believers and servants of the kingdom of the Father. The Master reminded them that his presence and sojourning with them come to an end, for him to return to the Father in heaven. The Master reminded them that before he was arrested, he had told them many times that the Jewish rulers and high priests would deliver him and put him to death. "But on the third day I will rise from the tomb." But most of you felt disconcerted and doubtful about my resurrection. You failed to believe me because you clearly did not understand the whole meaning of all this phenomenon.

Now, all of you must fully comprehend the true and real meaning of my sojourn on earth with you, to reveal the love, mercy, and the absolutely all-wise will of the Father. I revealed to you that you are all the children of God, and by fully submitting to the divine will of the Father and being born again of the spirit, you will all attain to be the children of light and life by fully abiding by the gospel of the kingdom. Then you will ascend on high in progression until you will be with me and the Father in Paradise.

Jesus continued by saying, "As I always told you, love all your fellowmen as I have loved you; serve them as I serve you. Spread the gospel of the kingdom throughout the whole world. Share the love of the Father with all the races of the world. I will always be with you, with the Spirit of Truth that I will send to you, who will continue to guide and protect you. My peace I leave with you."

When the Master finished speaking, he vanished from their sight. It was almost daybreak when the believers dispersed after they had digested all the admonitions, sermons, and teachings of the Master.

THE APPEARANCE AT SYCHAR

Paper 193:1

About four o'clock on Sabbath afternoon, May 13, the Master appeared to Nalda and about seventy-five Samaritan believers near Jacob's well at Sychar. The believers were in the habit of meeting at this place, near where Jesus had spoken to Nalda concerning the water of life. On this day, just as they had finished their discussions of the reported resurrection, Jesus suddenly appeared before them, saying:

The Samaritan believers meet near Jacob's well on a regular basis. Today, they are discussing the story of Jesus' crucifixion, death, and resurrection. When they finished their discussion, Jesus suddenly appeared before them, saying his usual greeting, "Peace be upon you." Jesus continued by saying, "I am the resurrection and the life. You have to have an unwavering faith in the Universal Father, and then be born of the eternal spirit, and be the children of the loving God and gain salvation into eternal life. The Universal Father does not ask anything from us but to believe in him, obey him, and have absolute faith in him."

Jesus continues by emphasizing the doctrine of the Fatherhood of God and the Brotherhood of mankind. This means that if you consider your brethren as your brother, you will treat your fellow human being like a brother or sister, giving them brotherly and sisterly love.

The Samaritans were so greatly impressed by the appearance and teaching of Jesus that they did not waste time in spreading the good news to the nearby towns. This was the seventeenth appearance of the Master.

THE PHOENICIAN APPEARANCE

Paper 193:2

The Master's eighteenth morontia appearance was at Tyre, on Tuesday, May 16, at a little before nine o'clock in the evening. Again, he appeared at the close of the meeting of believers, as they were about to disperse, saying:

"Peace be upon you."

I know that you feel the joy in your hearts knowing that the Son of Man has risen from the dead, and you will all experience this when the time comes for you to embrace eternal life. But remember that eternal life is only given to those who hunger and seek for truth, righteousness, and are born of the spirit, possessing absolute faith in the Universal Father.

Jesus admonished the believers to go out and preach the Fatherhood of God and the brotherhood and sisterhood of mankind to the world. The spirit-born and God-loving mortal must possess these attributes and feelings: loving service, unselfish devotion, courageous loyalty, sincere fairness, enlightened honesty, undying hope, confiding trust, merciful ministry, unfailing goodness, forgiving tolerance, and enduring peace.

If the professed believers bear not these fruits of the divine spirit in their lives, they are dead; the Spirit of Truth is not in them they are useless branches. The Father in heaven requires that the children of faith must bear much fruit of the Spirit, or else they will be taken out. You must strive to be fruitful and abundant in spiritual growth.

The Father said, "You may enter the kingdom as a child, but you must grow up and gain full spiritual maturity. I will be with you always in spreading the gospel of the kingdom, and the Spirit of Truth will always be with you, and my peace I leave with you."

Then the Master disappeared from their sight. From Tyre, the believers went to Sidon, Antioch, and Damascus to spread the good news of the Master's resurrection.

LAST APPEARANCE IN JERUSALEM

Paper 193:3

Early Thursday morning, May 18, Jesus made his last appearance on earth as a morontia personality. As the eleven apostles were about to sit down to breakfast in the upper chamber of Mary Mark's home, Jesus appeared to them and said:

"Peace be upon you," Jesus said that after he has gone to the Father, he will pour out the spirit of truth to all mankind. You will be endowed with the power and wisdom from above. Simon Zelotes interrupted Jesus, then asked, "Master, will you restore the kingdom, and are we going to see the glory of God manifested on earth?"

After Jesus listened to Simon's questions, full of false hope and expectations, the Master answered, "Simon, you still cling to the idea of a Jewish Messiah and a material kingdom. The belief of the Jews is that there will be a very special, powerful, and strong man from the Jewish clan someone like David who will become the Jewish deliverer, savior, and messiah of all the Jewish people on earth. And he will establish a Jewish kingdom on earth, which will be the most powerful kingdom on earth."

Jesus clarified that these beliefs are misguided and totally untrue. The Universal Father already has a Heavenly Kingdom the Isle of Paradise and its billions of heavenly spheres, with billions and trillions of spiritual kinds of angels, coordinates, and associates.

The Universal Father sends sons and daughters from heavenly spheres to the material worlds to teach, enlighten, and reveal his will to the people of the worlds. Around thirty-seven thousand years ago, he sent the material son and daughter (Adam and Eve) to teach, educate, and civilize the primitive people on earth during those periods. Adam and Eve are from Jerusem (a heavenly sphere). Their origin is spirit, and they were rematerialized as humans when they arrived on earth.

Then, during Abraham's era, around 2,000 years ago, the Magisterial Son (Machiventa Melchizedek) was sent to earth. After dematerialization, Melchizedek suddenly appeared in the tent of a Chaldean herder named Amdon. The herder was shocked and astonished. Melchizedek announced that he is the priest of El Elyon, the Most High, the one and only God. When Amdon, the herder, recovered from the shock, he invited Melchizedek to eat supper with him in his tent.

Melchizedek stayed on earth for almost one hundred years, teaching and proclaiming one supreme

God of the universe. He was the High Priest of Salem. Machiventa Melchizedek was originally a spiritual being, a Magisterial Son.

Then, after Melchizedek, the Creator Son (Christ Michael), Jesus Christ, was sent to the world as revealer, teacher, and savior of the world. The origin of Christ Michael is the spirit. He is the Creator Son who created the local universe of ten million inhabited planets.

The Universal Father sends teachers, revealers, educators, saviors, and enlighteners to the world to show the world the true attributes, nature, and character of God. They all have a spiritual origin. I do not think God will make a particular man or woman of mortal being origin to be a messiah or a king and savior.

THE MASTER'S ASCENSION

Paper 193:5

It was almost half past seven o'clock this Thursday morning, May 18, when Jesus arrived on the western slope of Mount Olivet with his eleven silent, somewhat bewildered apostles.

This is the day that the Master will finally ascend to his Father in heaven. The eleven apostles are present at this final appearance and ascension of the Master. About two-thirds of the way up to the very top of the mountain, they can see down to Jerusalem and Gethsemane. As Jesus stood while all the apostles were around him, the Master spoke:

"I bade you to tarry in Jerusalem until you were endowed with power on high. I am now about to take leave of you; I am about to ascend to my Father, and soon we will send to this world the Spirit of Truth. You will begin to proclaim the gospel of the kingdom from Jerusalem to the end of the world. Love everyone as I have loved you; serve your fellow human as I served you. Remember all the things that I have taught you. My love overshadows you, my spirit will dwell with you, and my peace shall abide upon you. Farewell."

Then the Master disappeared from their sight. This disappearance of Jesus and his ascension on high is the same as when Jesus appeared and disappeared from the sight of the people.

The Master's ascension journey was by way of Jerusem, where the Most Highs, under the observation of the Paradise Son, released Jesus of Nazareth from the morontia state and, through the spirit channels of ascension, reinstated him to the status of Paradise sonship and as the supreme sovereign of Salvington (the local universe).

CONCLUSION

The world must understand that when our mortal body of flesh and blood dies, it will completely perish and return to the dust from which it came. But we all have a soul, personality, and spirit unlike animals, who have material bodies but do not possess a soul, personality, and spirit. That is why, even though there are billions of human beings on earth, each of us has a unique personality that differs from the others. Even twins have different personalities, traits, and characteristics.

Christian believers believe that Jesus' resurrection was material that Jesus' body of flesh and blood is the one that came back from the dead and resurrected, and that the body of flesh and blood of Jesus ascended to heaven. As I have pointed out, if Jesus' dead body after the crucifixion had been burned (cremated), fed to wild animals, or thrown down a pit and eaten by wild beasts, there would be no material body of Jesus to resurrect.

Christ Michael is spirit; he dwells in spiritual realms. Heavenly spheres are the homes of spiritual beings there can never be a material mortal with a body of flesh and blood that can survive in the heavenly spheres.

Christ Michael used the mortal body of Jesus of Nazareth on earth from birth to reveal to the world the will of the Father in heaven. After Christ Michael, inside the material body of Jesus, had finished his mission on earth, he ascended again to heaven as a spirit being and returned to his original status as the sovereign God of the local universe and the Spirit Son of God.

About The Author

I am a born believer, but when I reached the age of 50s I became more interested in knowing more about God, and all the whole universe creations.

I read the Bible, Koran, and Hebrew scriptures. But I am asking questions about some of the written scriptures in all the books.

But when I read the Urantia Book, it answered all the questions and mysteries about God, the Universe and Universes, its creations, evolutions, cosmology, science, and philosophy.

www.ingramcontent.com/pod-product-compliance
Lightning Source LLC
Chambersburg PA
CBHW041126120626
46547CB00019B/2868